Howdy, Fellow Artists!

This is Farmer Ralph, welcoming you to my book on how to draw things found on a farm. I have great admiration for farmers. They are tough, hard-working folks who tend and grow all kinds of things that we need to live. Without farmers and farms, where would our food come from?

In this book I will show you simple ways to draw common barnyard animals. You'll also learn how to draw hay bales, a tractor, a farmer, and a barn.

Carefully follow the steps in red to create your own farm drawings. Use the challenge steps in blue to add more character and detail. And remember . . . have fun!

Ralph

Choose your tools

pastel pencil • crayon • watercolor • fine-tip marker • colored pencil • marker • poster paint

Baby Chicks

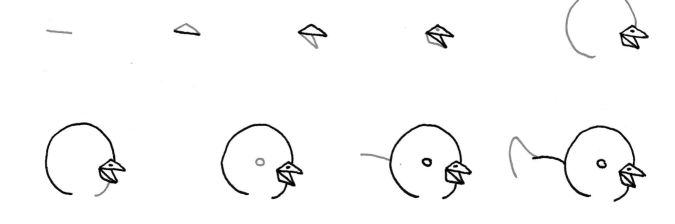

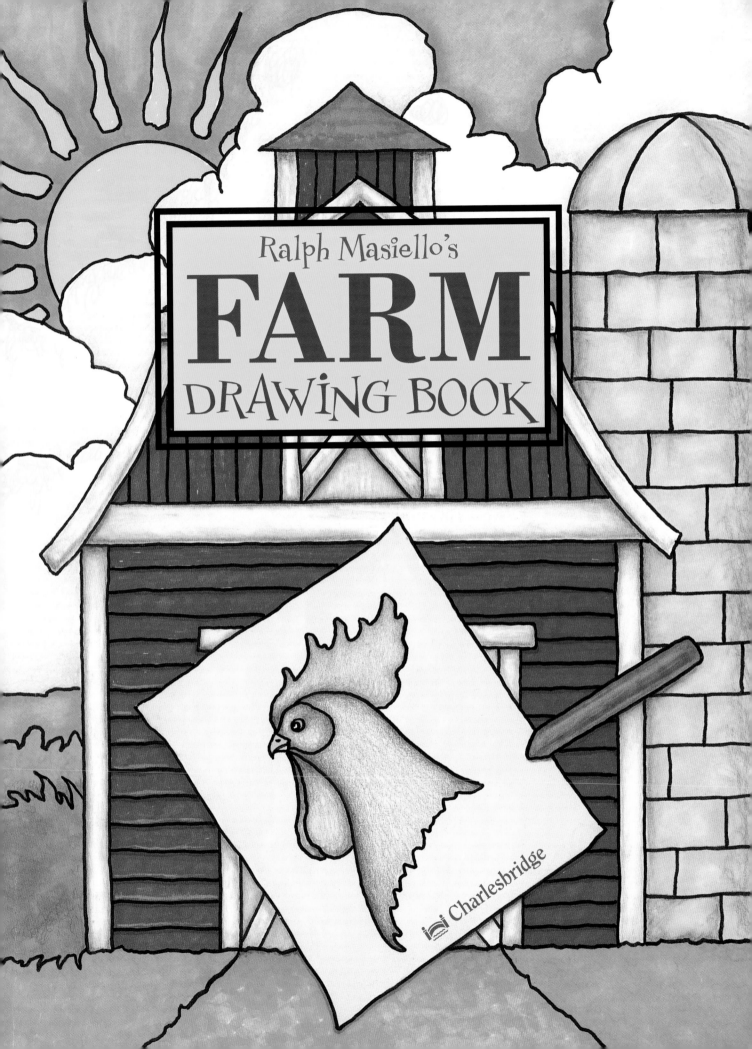

To all those who work with earth to supply our Earth with food—R. M.

In this series:

Ralph Masiello's Ancient Egypt Drawing Book

Ralph Masiello's Bug Drawing Book

Ralph Masiello's Christmas Drawing Book

Ralph Masiello's Dinosaur Drawing Book

Ralph Masiello's Dragon Drawing Book

Ralph Masiello's Fairy Drawing Book

Ralph Masiello's Farm Drawing Book

Ralph Masiello's Halloween Drawing Book

Ralph Masiello's Ocean Drawing Book

Ralph Masiello's Robot Drawing Book

Other books illustrated by Ralph Masiello:

The Dinosaur Alphabet Book

The Extinct Alphabet Book

The Flag We Love

The Frog Alphabet Book

The Icky Bug Alphabet Book

The Icky Bug Counting Book

The Mystic Phyles: Beasts

The Skull Alphabet Book

The Yucky Reptile Alphabet Book

Cuenta los insectos

Published by Charlesbridge
85 Main Street
Watertown, MA 02472
(617) 926-0329
www.charlesbridge.com

Library of Congress Cataloging-in-Publication Data
Masiello, Ralph.
    Ralph Masiello's farm drawing book / Ralph Masiello.
        p. cm.
    ISBN 978-1-57091-537-6 (reinforced for library use)
    ISBN 978-1-57091-538-3 (softcover)
    ISBN 978-1-60734-082-9 (ebook pdf)
1. Domestic animals in art—Juvenile literature. 2. Livestock in art—Juvenile literature.
3. Drawing—Technique—Juvenile literature. I. Title.
NC783.8.D65M37 2012
743.6—dc22   2011004024

Printed in China
(hc) 10 9 8 7 6 5 4 3 2 1
(sc) 10 9 8 7 6 5 4 3 2

Illustrations done in mixed media
Display type set in Couchlover, designed by Chank, Minneapolis, Minnesota;
    text type set in Goudy
Color separations by KHL Chroma Graphics, Singapore
Printed by Jade Productions in Heyuan, Guangdong, China
Production supervision by Brian G. Walker
Designed by Susan Mallory Sherman and Martha MacLeod Sikkema

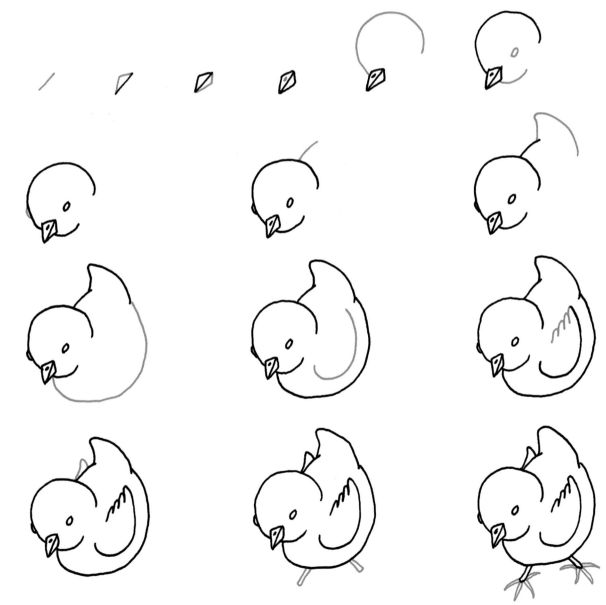

Hen

Rooster

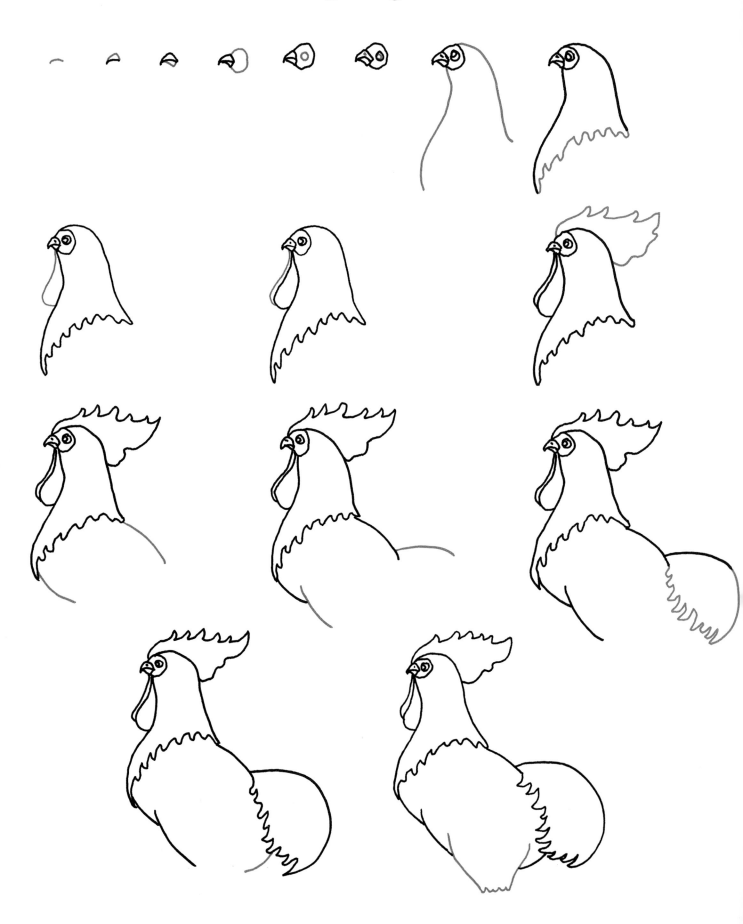

What clucky parents to have such cute chicks!

Try to overlap the shapes of the chicks.

crayon

Pig

You're such a ham.

colored pencil

Grass and Hills

Billy Goat

This billy goat's not so gruff.

marker and pastel pencil

Flower (Daisy)

Dairy Cow

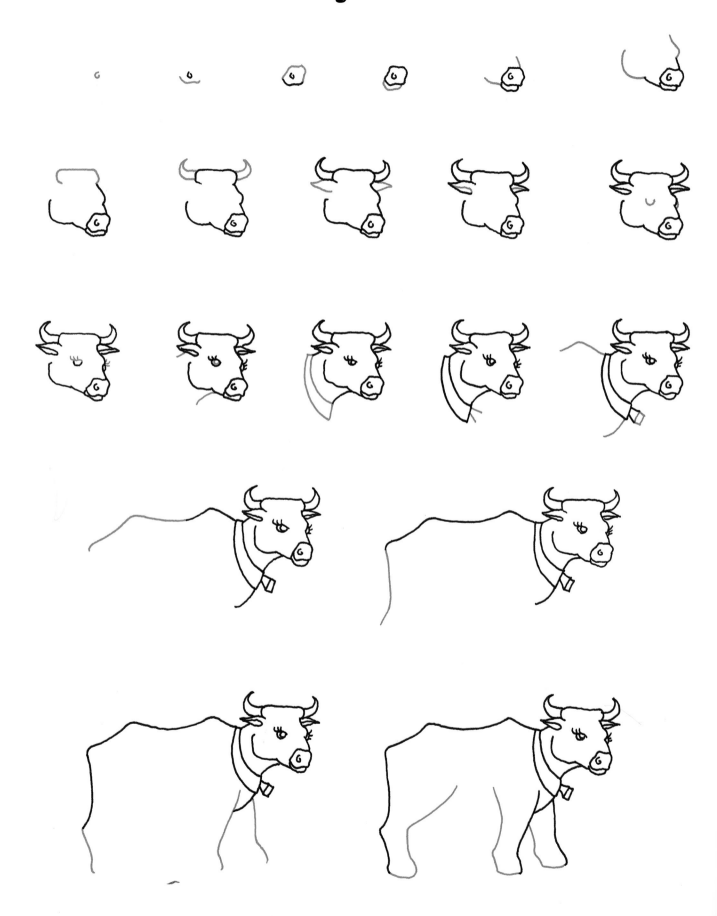

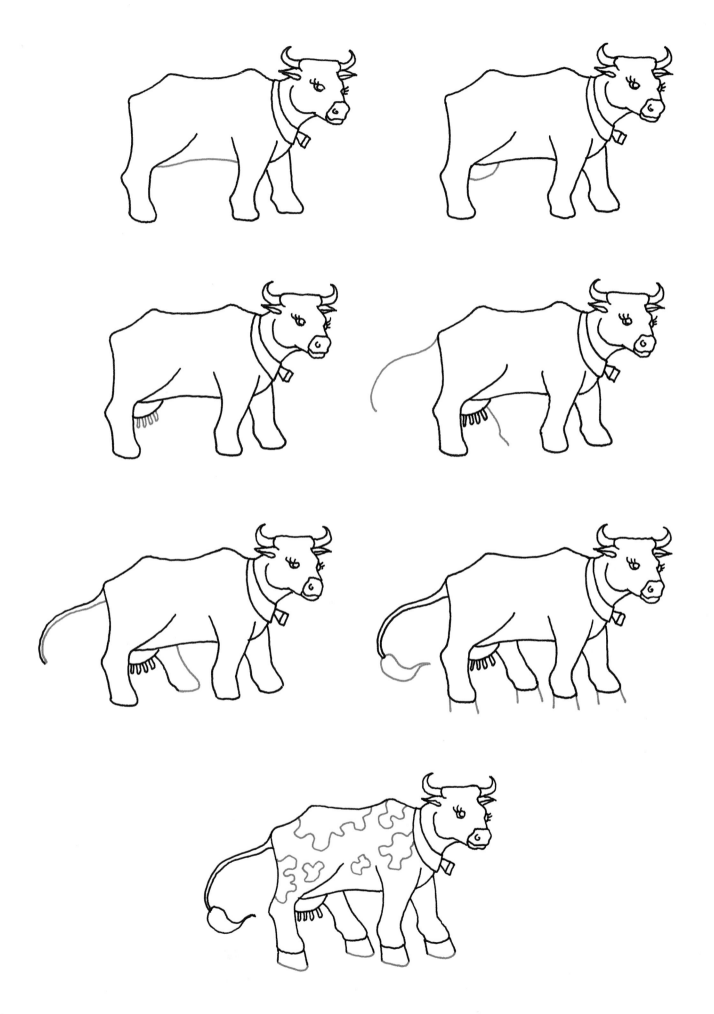

Stacked Hay Bales

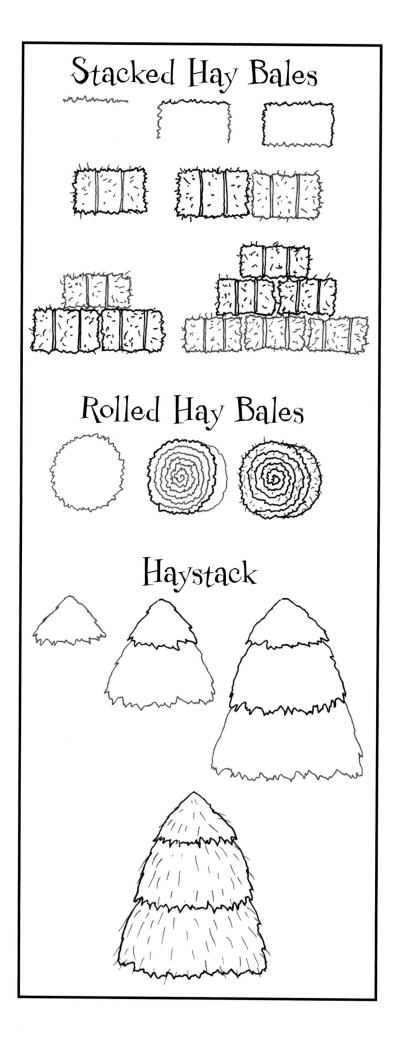

Rolled Hay Bales

Haystack

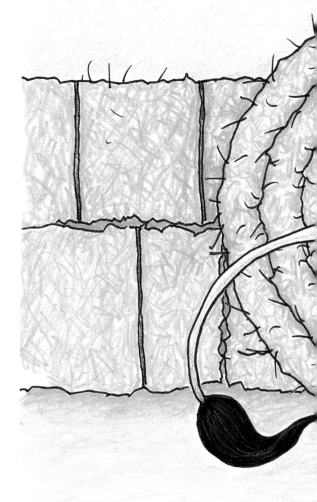

Hey! How about some hay?

marker and colored pencil

Horse

Put your best hoof forward!

marker and colored pencil

High-stepping Horse

Farmer and Tractor

Barn

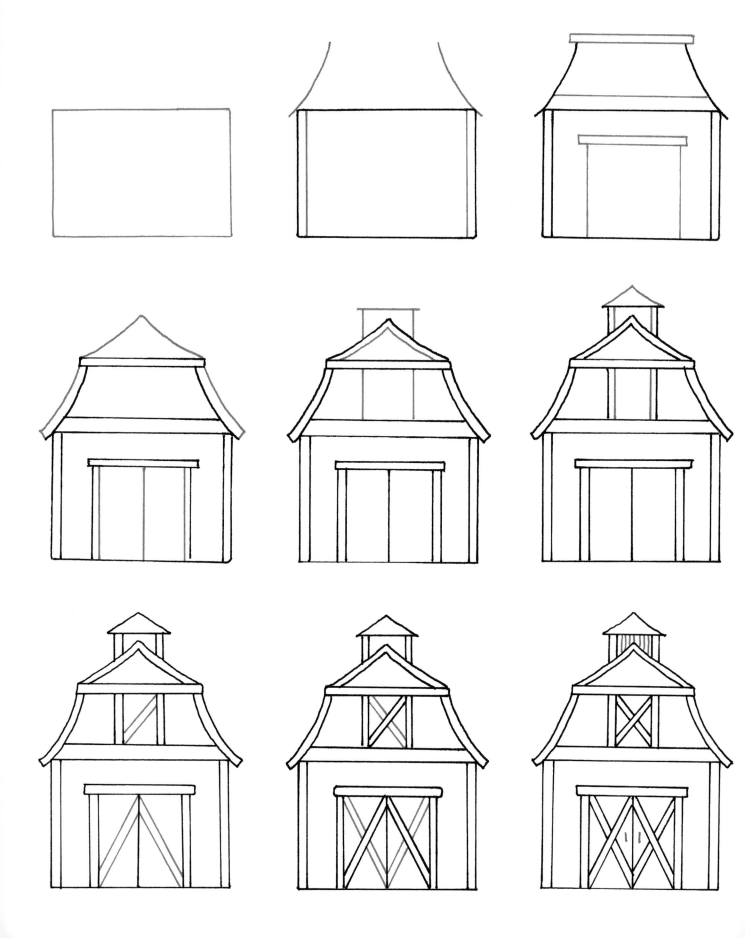

Add a silo.

Add some bushes.

Add a fence.

Add some clouds.

And the sun.

And a welcoming road.

Old MacDonald drew a farm!

Resources

Now that you have drawn some great farm pictures, why not learn more about farm life? Here are some books and websites all about farms. Some are informative, some have crafts, and some are just plain fun. Enjoy!

Books

Artley, Bob. *Once Upon a Farm*. Gretna, LA: Pelican, 2000.

Cronin, Doreen. *Giggle, Giggle, Quack*. New York: Atheneum, 2002.

Ehlert, Lois. *Color Farm*. New York: HarperCollins, 1990.

Farm. Ultimate Sticker Books. New York: DK Publishing, 2004.

Krosoczka, Jarrett J. *Punk Farm*. New York: Knopf, 2005.

Macaulay, David. *Black and White*. Boston: Houghton Mifflin, 1990.

Rosen, Michael J. *Our Farm: Four Seasons with Five Kids on One Family's Farm*. Plain City, OH: Darby Creek, 2008.

White, E. B. *Charlotte's Web*. New York: Harper & Brothers, 1952.

Wiesner, David. *The Three Pigs*. New York: Clarion Books, 2001.

Websites

Websites can change. Try running a search for *farm* on your favorite search engine.

Barnyard Palace
www.ncagr.gov/cyber/kidswrld/general/barnyard/barnyard.htm
Click on an aerial view of a farm to find out more about its animals.

CanTeach: Songs & Poems: On the Farm
www.canteach.ca/elementary/songspoems55.html
Already know *Old MacDonald Had a Farm*? Try these other songs and poems about farms.

4-H Virtual Farm
www.sites.ext.vt.edu/virtualfarm/main.html
Explore farms that raise horses, dairy cows, cattle, poultry, and even fish.

All About Farm Animals
www.kiddyhouse.com/Farm
Find fun facts and activities about ducks, sheep, turkeys, cows, and other farm animals.

The Teacher's Guide: On the Farm
www.theteachersguide.com/onthefarm.htm
Teachers: Enrich a farm unit with activities, PowerPoint presentations, printouts, and clip art.